The NATIONAL CURRICULUM

A Survival Guide for Parents

Ruth Merttens and Jeff Vass
Co-Directors of the IMPACT Project

CONTENTS

INTRODUCTION

What is The National Curriculum?

In 1988 Parliament passed the Education Reform Act which will bring about the biggest changes to the education system in England and Wales since 1945. An important aspect of this change is to the curriculum which is **what children are taught or learn at school.**

Up until 1988, although England and Wales had a national system of exams – GCSEs at 16 for everyone, and an 11+ in some areas – the subjects each school covered, and in what order, was left largely to the individual schools and Local Education Authorities to decide.

With the passing of the 1988 Education Reform Act (**ERA**), much of this choice was removed from schools and Local Education Authorities. From now on, all schools, except those in the private sector, will have to follow the same curriculum. The content of the curriculum – what subjects are taught, which parts of each subject and so on – is now laid down by law. Scotland now has its own version of the National Curriculum, as does Northern Ireland.

The National Curriculum is an **entitlement** for every child. All children in England and Wales, no matter what city or county they live in, or which schools they attend will therefore follow the same curriculum and learn the same basic things.

The National Curriculum is built around a system of **assessment**. Almost every subject the children are to study is divided into 10 levels. The children progress up the 10 rungs on this ladder within each subject as they move through their schooling. This progress is monitored stage by stage. All children will be assessed throughout their education unless they have a statement of special needs. This may exempt a child from some or all of the National Curriculum. Every school will have to administer assessment to record the progress of each child. Every child's progress in each subject area will be assessed both by the teacher and by a series of *Standard Assessment Tasks (SATs).*

Children will be assessed continuously to ensure that they are progressing satisfactorily in all subjects. However, at certain *Key Reporting Stages*, the results of these assessments will be reported back to parents and to the wider community. These Key Reporting Stages are at ages 7, 11, 14 and 16.

When will the National Curriculum be introduced in schools?

The timetable for the phasing-in of the National Curriculum and its related assessment programme is now as follows:

Summer 1991	The children who have reached the end of Key Stage 1 (7 year olds) will be assessed on the *Core subjects* – maths, English and science. This is an officially unreported assessment, but parents will be entitled to receive a full report on their child.
Autumn 1991	The history and geography parts of the National Curriculum must officially be taught in all schools to children from age 5 to age 14.
Summer 1992	Children at the end of Key Stage 1 (7 year olds) will be assessed in the Core subjects – maths, English and science. It is possible that technology will also be assessed. The results of these assessments will be fully reported. Children at the end of Key Stage 3 (14 year olds) will also be assessed in maths and science. These results will not be officially reported, but parents will be entitled to a full report on their child.
Autumn 1992	The curriculum in maths, science and English for Key Stage 4 will have been decided, and children of 14 will embark upon the new *Programmes of Study.* The modern languages, music, art and physical education parts of the National Curriculum will be taught to children to whom they apply in Key Stages 1, 2 and 3.
Summer 1993	Children at the end of Key Stage 3 (14 year olds) will be assessed in maths, science, technology and English.

Do not worry if some of the terms and ideas used in this introduction are unfamiliar. The rest of this book sets out in detail the various aspects of the curriculum and explains new concepts and terms. Where examples are given, we have focused on the primary school curriculum, but the general explanations and guidelines are applicable to the introduction of the National Curriculum in either primary or secondary schools.

THE STRUCTURE OF THE NATIONAL CURRICULUM

The subjects of the National Curriculum

There are ten subjects in the National Curriculum; three of these – maths, English and science – are known as Core subjects. (See pages 14-20 for an outline of each Core subject, and pages 21-23 for details of the *Foundation subjects*).

Core Subjects

Maths	English	Science

Other Foundation Subjects

Geography	History	Technology	Art	Music	PE	Modern Foreign Language

In Wales, Welsh is a Core subject in Welsh speaking schools and a Foundation subject in other schools.

The content of each subject in the National Curriculum is outlined in a specially produced document. These were produced by a panel of experts, and were then subject to consultation and revision. The final documents present what is to be taught in each subject area.

These documents are necessarily very detailed. In order to simplify the process, they are all presented in the same way. Each subject is divided into *Attainment Targets* (ATs). ATs can best be thought of as bundles of related skills or facts. These are the knowledge, understanding and skills children need in one particular part of a subject.

The Attainment Targets in the three Core Curriculum subjects.

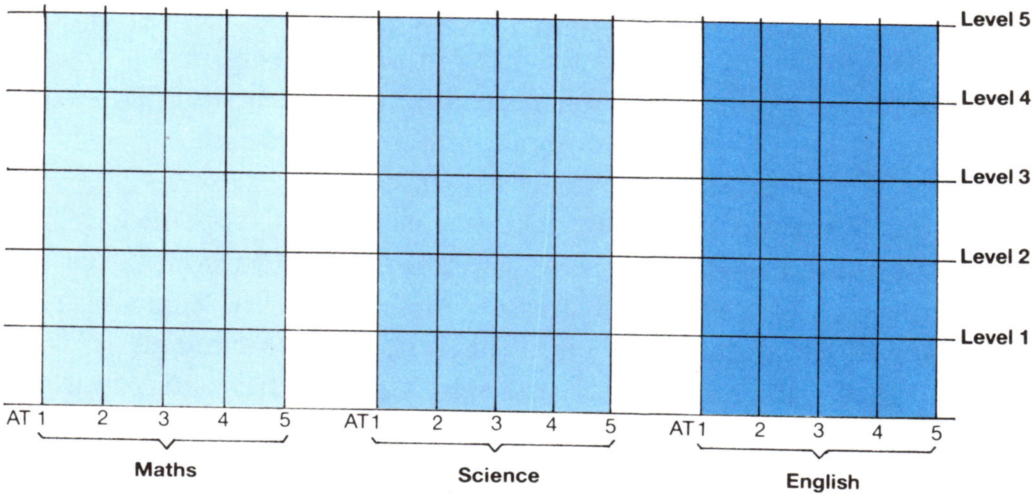

Are these ATs now here for ever?

No. At the time of writing there are 5 proposed ATs in Maths, 5 proposed ATs in Science and 5 ATs in English. However, at any time, the content of the subject documents may be revised by the government. This means that what is required to be taught in maths or in any other subject, can be adapted or updated if required.

Levels of Attainment

Each Attainment Target is divided into ten *Levels of Attainment*. These define the stages through which children are expected to pass as they progress through the curriculum in each Attainment Target i.e. in each part of each subject, the Level of Attainment describes precisely what a child should know or the skills he or she must possess in order to be said to have reached that level (see pages 12-13 for more about the Levels of Attainment).

Teaching the National Curriculum

The National Curriculum specifies which subjects are to be taught in schools at each Key Stage. It does not specify the amount of time a teacher is to spend on any one subject. However the assessment procedures will themselves ensure that all teachers give appropriate amounts of time to each subject.

In primary schools most time is spent in acquiring knowledge, skills and understanding in the three Core subjects: English, maths and science. Therefore many teachers feel that the other Foundation subjects of history, geography and so on can best be taught largely in the context of the work already in progress in the Core subjects, although they could be taught as separate subjects if the head and governors so decide. This reinforces what the Government and Her Majesty's Inspectors of Schools (HMIs) see as good teaching in primary schools. Teachers will need to plan the curriculum **as a whole**. History or geography can be taught using mathematical knowledge, practising writing skills, reading and so on (see pages 21-23).

The National Curriculum means that the subjects children are taught are laid down by law. Therefore it should not matter whether a child lives in Nottingham, in Gwent or in Peckham, he or she will be studying the same subjects, and the same areas within those subjects, at the same stages as all other children in England and Wales. It is also the case that one child can progress faster through the curriculum than another; there is room for different children to progress at their own rates.

Although all children are entitled to the National Curriculum, it may be necessary to make exceptional arrangements for some children and to modify the curriculum to suit their requirements. This is envisaged as a rare rather than a common occurrence as the curriculum incorporates a great deal of flexibility as to the level of work children study at one age. It is a guiding principle of the curriculum that children with special educational needs experience as far as possible the full range of the curriculum.

Profile Components

The National Curriculum divides up each subject into Attainment Targets or bundles of related skills, and the Attainment Targets are themselves grouped into *Profile Components*. Each subject can now be simplified as seen below:

The Profile Components of the three Core Curriculum subjects.

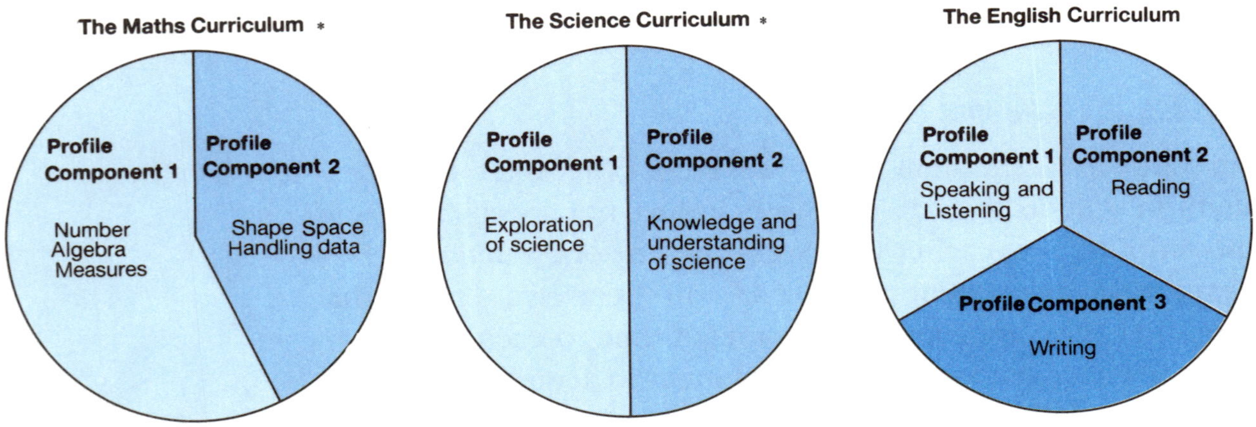

**This is currently subject to change by S.E.A.C.*

Each Profile Component lists the knowledge, skills and understanding which a child must have in order to progress through that part of the National Curriculum.

What is the point of Profile Components? Don't they complicate the process?

The main purpose of dividing each subject into separate Profile Components is that it makes it much **easier** for information about a child's progress to be given to parents and discussed. Although teachers need to consider all the different parts of each subject in great detail in order to plan the children's work, parents simply need to understand how their child is progressing in each area of each subject.

Will it be easier to discuss my child's progress with her teachers after the introduction of the National Curriculum?

It is probable that both parents and teachers will want to discuss each child's learning in terms of his or her progress in each Profile Component. For example, Mary's mother may receive a teacher's report under such headings as:

ENGLISH

Profile Component 1 (Speaking and Listening)

Mary: Level 1
Class Attainment: Level 1 - 2 children
Level 2 - 20 children
Level 3 - 8 children

Additional Information: Mary lacks confidence in this area. She is reluctant to speak in front of a group. When she is persuaded to speak, she frequently resorts to repeating what the last speaker just said. Mary gives the appearance of being an attentive listener but in fact her thoughts are often far away from what the speaker is saying.

Profile Component 2 (Reading)

Mary: Level 3
Class Attainment: Level 1 - 5 children
Level 2 - 21 children
Level 3 - 4 children

Additional Information: Mary is an able reader, and as one of the most fluent readers in the class, she is considerably ahead of the stage expected at her age. She can also take in and respond well to a story being read to her which is intended for much older children. She shows great empathy with the characters and a good understanding of plot.

Profile Component 3 (Writing)

Mary: Level 2
Class Attainment: Level 1 - 7 children
Level 2 - 22 children
Level 3 - 1 child

Additional Information: Mary is progressing well and takes more care forming and in separating words from each other. What she writes is always interesting and imaginatively expressed. She seems to have no lack of ideas.

MATHEMATICS

*This is currently subject to change

Profile Component 1 (Number and Algebra*)

Mary: Level 2
Class Attainment: Level 1 - 3 children
Level 2 - 20 children
Level 3 - 7 children

Additional Information: Mary is more than average in her familiarity with numbers. She is competent at adding and subtracting numbers under 20 and can attempt some quite hard sums. She is already familiar with quite a few standard units of measurement and is especially advanced in being able to tell the time.

Profile Component 2 (Shape, Space and Handling Data*)

Mary: Level 1
Class Attainment: Level 1 - 5 children
Level 2 - 18 children
Level 3 - 7 children

Additional Information: Mary had real difficulty in this area. Her spatial awareness is very poor and she is often unable to explain where one thing is, in relation to another. She is quite good at understanding displays of information such as simple graphs and diagrams. Her numeracy is an advantage here.

In Summary

The National Curriculum will give teachers and parents a common language in which to discuss children's progress. Profile Components, or broad areas within each subject, will make it very easy to talk about each aspect of a child's development in terms which make sense to both parents and teachers.

ASSESSMENT

From the time of the introduction of the National Curriculum, it will be every teacher's job to ensure that all the children in her class are regularly monitored to find out what they have learned so far, and whether or not they are progressing. The purpose of this is to diagnose any problems or learning difficulties a child is experiencing which can be recognised early so that more help can be provided where it is needed.

At the end of each Key Stage of the National Curriculum, children will be assessed to see at what level they are working in each of the Core subjects. They may also be assessed on some or all of the Foundation subjects.

The Key Stages

Key Stage 1: Applies to children aged 5-7 years of age.
Includes:
- Reception – 4/5 year olds
- Year 1 (Y1) – 5/6 year olds
- Year 2 (Y2) – 6/7 year olds

Key Stage 2: Applies to children aged 7-11 years of age.
Includes:
- Year 3 (Y3) – 7/8 year olds
- Year 4 (Y4) – 8/9 year olds
- Year 5 (Y5) – 9/10 year olds
- Year 6 (Y6) – 10/11 year olds

Key Stage 3: Applies to children aged 11-14 years of age.
Includes:
- Year 7 (Y7) – 11/12 year olds
- Year 8 (Y8) – 12/13 year olds
- Year 9 (Y9) – 13/14 year olds

Key Stage 4: Applies to children aged 14-16 years of age.
Includes:
- Year 10 (Y10) – 14/15 year olds
- Year 11 (Y11) – 15/16 year olds

At the end of each Key Stage children are assessed and the results will be reported to parents.

Each child will be assessed using a combination of Standard Assessment Tasks (SATS) and the class teacher's own *Continuous Assessment.* The SATs will be supplied by a government appointed agency and all schools must choose from the same bank of them. Both the teacher's assessment and the Standard Assessment Tasks will be used to show where each child is on the 10 level ladder in all subjects at the four Key Reporting Stages.

What is the point of all this assessment?

Assessment plays a much more important role in education under the National Curriculum. Each Key Stage has its own Programme of Study (**what** the children have to learn) and its own assessment at the end. The assessments at the end of Key Stages 1, 2 and 3 will all involve two parts:

1. The Teacher's Assessment

This is like a combination of Continuous Assessment and the reports which teachers used to write at the end of the year or term. Teachers are required to produce a detailed record of each child's performance on every Attainment Target in the Core subjects.This assessment is based on the work children have produced over the course of the year, and the teacher's professional observation of the children's performance. For example, a teacher will save some of the work children do in their maths books or folders. She will also have made notes on how they get on when they are doing an activity which requires them to count or add up, etc.

Every child will therefore be given a 'score' for each aspect of the Core subjects. Eg. a child might be at level 2 on AT2 (Number) and a level 1 on AT3 (Algebra). The teacher's final record will show each level on each Attainment Target.

Teachers may assess children on the Foundation subjects, including technology. Methods for recording these subjects will also be provided.

These records must be completed by the beginning of the summer term at the end of each Key Stage. This is when children are 7 or nearly 7 years old, when they are 11, or nearly 11 years old, when they are 14 and when they are 16.

2. The Standard Assessment Tasks

Every school will be supplied with Standard Assessment Tasks (SATs). These are produced by the Schools Examination and Assessment Council (S.E.A.C.) who are responsible for the National Curriculum assessment arrangements. The children must do these tasks in the first half of the summer term at the end of a Key Stage – i.e. at 7, 11, and 14 as listed in the preceding paragraph. The results of these are then combined with the results of the teacher assessment to produce a final score for each child on every part of the National Curriculum Core subjects, and in some cases, on the *Foundation subjects* as well. At present the tests have only been produced for Key Stage 1 – the rest are in the development phase.

For Key Stage 1, the Standard Assessment Tasks (SATs) will consist of a series of standardised tasks which teachers will administer in accordance with the instructions supplied. The tasks may take up to 30 hours of class time to administer and will be a part of the classwork over a period of a couple of weeks in the summer term.

What do the SATs test?

The SATs will not test every child's performance on every Attainment Target. This would be impossible! They will test certain **specified** ATs, including reading, writing, handwriting and spelling, using and applying mathematical skills, number work, and a knowledge of basic scientific processes.

What happens if the Teacher's Assessment differs from the results on the SATs?

In these cases, normally the SAT result will be taken and recorded as the final assessment outcome. However, in cases where the teacher believes that the child's performance is not adequately reflected in the test result, she can appeal to the moderation procedure to use the score from the Teacher's Assessment instead.

Will the SATs consist of written work only?

No. Certainly at Key Stage 1, the tests may involve speaking, listening, reading, using a computer, construction, drawing, and many other ways of working. The children will work together in groups for some of the tasks, and alone for others. At Key Stage 2, the tests may have a higher percentage of written work. By the time the children reach Key Stage 3, the tasks may have more in common with examinations, although this does not mean they will solely involve timed and written work.

Reporting the results

Parents are always entitled to know the results of all the assessments of their child. The assessment results will be collated to give the overall results for the whole class, and for the whole school. As the National Curriculum is phased in, these overall figures will also be reported to parents, governors and the whole educational community.

While the new requirements will provide parents with a lot more information about their child's progress and about the school's performance, it is worth remembering that publishing a teacher's results – or a school's – may not help parents to make fair comparisons. The results after all, may be good or bad for reasons which have more to do with the intake of children or the resources supplied by parents, rather than the quality of teaching. For example a school in a social priority area or where the pupils are bilingual, may be extremely efficient, and possess gifted or committed teachers. However, its distribution of results may seem to be less impressive than a school in another area.

In Summary

Both parts of the assessment – the Teacher's Assessment and the SATs – will go towards getting a final result for each child in each profile component. Children will need to show that they are competent across a wide range of subjects and skills. Parents will receive a detailed report on their child's progress, and they will be able to make comparisons between their own child and the results for the class as a whole. This should give them a good idea of how their child is doing.

LEVELS OF ATTAINMENT

The curriculum is designed so that children can progress through each subject at their own rate. The important thing is that each child should make progress and not stand still or regress. In order to ensure that this happens each subject is described in 10 Levels of Attainment. These state the **criteria** which must be met for it to be said that a child has achieved a particular level.

LEVEL	STATEMENTS OF ATTAINMENT	EXAMPLE
2	• read accurately and understand straightforward signs, labels and notices.	*Read labels on drawers in the classroom; read simple menus.*
	• demonstrate knowledge of the alphabet in using word books and simple dictionaries.	*Turn towards the end to find words beginning with 's', rather than always starting from the beginning.*
	• use picture and context cues, words recognised on sight and phonic cues in reading.	*Use a picture to help make sense of a text; recognise that "Once" is often followed by "upon a time"; use initial letters to help with recognising words.*
	• describe what has happened in a story and predict what may happen next.	*Talk about how and why Jack climbs the beanstalk and suggest what may be at the top.*
	• listen and respond to stories, poems and other material read aloud, expressing opinions informed by what has been read.	*Talk about characters, their actions and appearance; discuss the behaviour of different animals described in a radio programme.*
	• read a range of material with some independence, fluency, accuracy and understanding.	*Read something unprompted; talk with some confidence about what has been read; produce craftwork related to reading work.*

Example showing the criteria which a child must meet for English Attainment Target 2: Reading at level 2.

What are the criteria for the 10 Levels of Attainment?

It is easiest to describe this aspect of the National Curriculum using the example of a driving test. To pass a driving test, it is not sufficient simply to be as good as the average driver in your area. It is necessary to demonstrate that **you** possess particular **specified** skills. The examiner will not be looking to see if you are as good a driver as Joe Bloggs, he will be looking down a list of skills – or criteria – and measuring your performance against these: for example, do you look in your mirror at regular intervals? Can you do an emergency stop? It is only if your driving meets all the required criteria that the examiner will agree that you have passed the test.

Under the National Curriculum teachers will know which criteria identify each stage or level in any one subject. They will be able to monitor a child's performance against these criteria in order to say what level the child has reached.

How do I know what level my child should be at?

Experts predict that 80% of all 7 year olds will be at Level 2. After this, it is expected that an average rate of progress would be to advance one further level with each two years of schooling.

Expected Rates of Progress.

Level	Approximate Ages
Level 5	11/12/13
Level 4	10/11/12
Level 3	8/9/10
Level 2	6/7/8
Level 1	4/5/6

In Summary

For the first time ever there will be nationally agreed criteria against which the progress of all children can be assessed. In theory, this means that it will be possible to compare one child's progress with the national averages. Certainly, in practice, it will mean that parents and teachers will have a way of looking at a child's progress in each subject. They will be able to make a realistic comparison between the level he or she has reached and that reached by the rest of the class.

CORE SUBJECTS

Maths

The Maths Curriculum is described in a Maths Curriculum document and it is this document that schools will use to plan each child's scheme of work in maths from the age of 5 onwards. There are 5 proposed Attainment Targets in maths – AT1, using and applying maths, AT2, number, AT3, algebra, AT4, shape and space and AT5, handling data.

Maths Attainment Targets

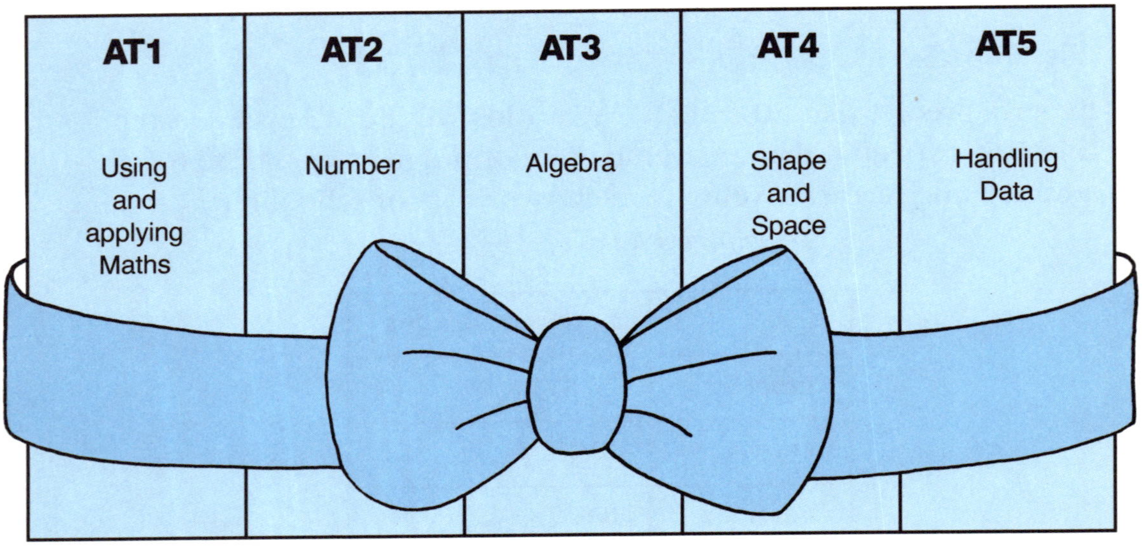

The first Attainment Target is special. It is concerned with the ability to use and apply maths in practical tasks and to solve real-life problems. This is very important since it affirms the idea that it is no use learning mathematical skills if you cannot apply them in everyday life.

As far as the assessment is concerned, the first attainment target is of particular importance.

Will children still learn the maths that parents remember?

The maths outlined in the National Curriculum is no surprise to anybody. The change is not so much in what maths the children learn, as in the approach taken to how they learn it. Emphasis is put upon children being able to apply what they have learned. They are expected to be able to use a particular skill, such as adding up, in a variety of situations.

Do children still need to know their times tables and so on?

Yes. Children will still be required to learn certain number facts. Attainment Target 2 covers understanding numbers, how they relate and so on, as well as adding, subtracting, multiplying and dividing.

LEVEL	STATEMENTS OF ATTAINMENT	EXAMPLE
3	• read, write and order numbers to at least 1000; use the knowledge that the position of a digit indicates its value.	*Know that 'four hundred and two' is written 402 and why neither 42 nor 4002 is correct.*
	• use decimal notation as the conventional way of recording in money.	*Know that three £1 coins plus six 1p coins is written as £3·06, and that 3·6 on a calculator means £3·60 in the context of money.*
	• appreciate the meaning of negative whole numbers in familiar contexts.	*Read a temperature scale; understand a negative output on a calculator.*

Example showing what children are required to understand for level 3 of Maths Attainment Target 2, Number.

However, some of the other Attainment Targets also require that children are able to relate one number fact to another, and understand the mathematical patterns involved. For example, at Level 3, Maths Attainment Target 1, Using and applying maths requires children to:

LEVEL	STATEMENTS OF ATTAINMENT	EXAMPLE
3	• use systematic methods of recording work and presenting results.	*Keep a record of wind direction over a period of time; display the results in an appropriate chart and discuss the findings.*
	• make a reasonable guess in order to start a task; know reasonableness of an answer.	*Guess how many linking cubes will be needed for each pupil in the class to have six.*
		Know when the answer given on a calculator is of the wrong order of magnitude.

Extract from Maths Attainment Target 1: Using and applying maths, Level 3.

Are calculators in or out of the National Curriculum?

Calculators are definitely in. It is vital that children in today's world learn how to use this important tool. It is also now recognised that calculators can play an important part in helping develop children's logical thinking and their use of strategies and mathematical techniques. Most of the jobs which our children will apply for will require that they can use a calculator with confidence and efficiency.

English

The English Curriculum is outlined in a separate document which describes in detail the 5 Attainment Targets in English. As with maths, these Attainment Targets are grouped into Profile Components. For the first two Key Stages of compulsory schooling, for children from 5 to 7 and 8 to 11 years of age, the Profile Components have **equal weighting**. That is to say each one is of equal importance when it comes to assessment.

English Profile Components.

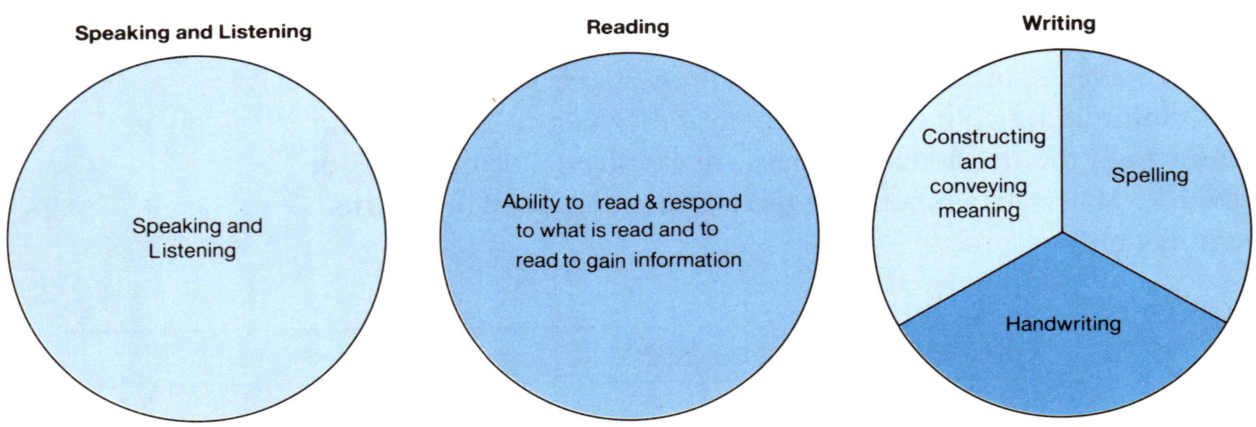

As seen in the diagram, speaking and listening is of equal importance as reading and writing and children will be assessed on their ability to listen, respond, discuss and articulate ideas as well as on their ability to read and write clearly. Teachers will therefore have to allow sufficient classroom time for children to work in groups, to discuss with and listen to other people – the ability to work collaboratively is stressed throughout the English Curriculum document.

LEVEL	STATEMENTS OF ATTAINMENT	EXAMPLE
2	• participate as speakers and listeners in a group engaged in a given task.	*Compose a story together; design and make a model; assume a role in play activity.*
	• describe an event, real or imagined, to the teacher or another pupil.	*Tell the listener about something which happened at home, on the television or in a book.*
	• listen attentively to stories and poems, and talk about them.	*Talk about the characters; say what they like or dislike about a story or poem.*
	• talk with the teacher, listen, and ask and answer questions.	*Talk about events or activities in or out of school – such as a school trip, a family outing or a television programme.*
	• respond appropriately to a range of more complex instructions given by a teacher, and give simple instructions.	*Follow three consecutive actions such as "Write down the place in the classroom where you think your plant will grow best, find out what the others on your table think and try to agree on which is likely to be the best place".*

This extract from English Attainment Target 1: Speaking and Listening, shows the importance of talk and discussion in the new curriculum.

Will children have to start learning "proper grammar" again?

Children of primary school age will **not** be taught the sentence grammar of English – noun, verb, adjective, etc. as a separate subject. However, such terms, along with many others relating to the structure of language e.g. vowel, consonant, syllable, apostrophe, comma, etc. will be taught when discussion of how language works, as well as what is being said, is appropriate. Children will need to be able to discuss how English works, how words fit together and how sense is constructed.

Will children be encouraged to learn Standard English?

The English document explicitly states that it is **the right** of all children, no matter what their first language, to be given the opportunity to acquire fluency in both written and spoken Standard English. The term 'Standard English' however refers to "grammar and vocabulary but **not** to accent". Therefore, children will not have to learn to speak with a uniform accent of intonation.

LEVEL	STATEMENTS OF ATTAINMENT	EXAMPLE
3	• produce, independently, pieces of writing using complete sentences, mainly demarcated with capital letters and full stops or question marks.	
	• shape chronological writing, beginning to use a wider range of sentence connectives than 'and' and 'then'.	*but when after so because*
	• write more complex stories with detail beyond simple events and with a defined ending.	*Stories which include a description of setting and the feelings of characters.*
	• produce a range of types of non-chronological writing.	*Plans and diagrams, descriptions of a person or place, or notes for an activity in science or design.*
	• begin to revise and redraft in discussion with the teacher, other adults, or other children in the class, paying attention to meaning and clarity as well as checking for matters such as correct and consistent use of tenses and pronouns.	

Example from English Attainment Target 3: Writing at level 3.

How will children be tested on reading?

The children will be assessed on reading in a variety of ways. The teacher keeps her own reading record of each child's progress. This enables her to make a judgement about what level the child is at. This is recorded on the Teacher Assessment form. In addition, part of the Standard Assessment Task addresses reading. A list of books is provided which are deemed to be at level 2, and at level 3. Each child will be required to read one of the books from this list. They have to answer questions about it and also their reading of particular passages is scrutinised in depth. This process is intended to provide a further score for the child.

Are the books on the list the best ones to read at home?

While there is no reason why parents should not read the books on the list for SATs, it would be silly to focus on those books in particular. The test specifically requires that children read a book with which they are **not** familiar, so any question of children 'learning' a book is precluded. Children need to read and enjoy a wide range of books. After all, we want them to grow up as readers, not just to pass a test.

Science

The first profile component in science, and the **only** one to be compulsorily tested by the SATs, concerns scientific processes. This means that, rather than focusing upon a huge body of knowledge or a large number of facts, young children are encouraged to explore and investigate, to build and test their own theories. They need to learn to describe and communicate their observations. The Programmes of Study also specify that children will need to work co-operatively in groups in order to achieve these aims.

The picture of children sitting in rows, working individually and learning facts from books is far from what the Science Curriculum implies. Children are expected to discover, through studying nature and the environment. They are required to examine living things – plants, animals and themselves. There is an emphasis on direct experience rather than knowledge acquired from books and facts to be stored.

The Science Curriculum is grouped into two Profile Components:

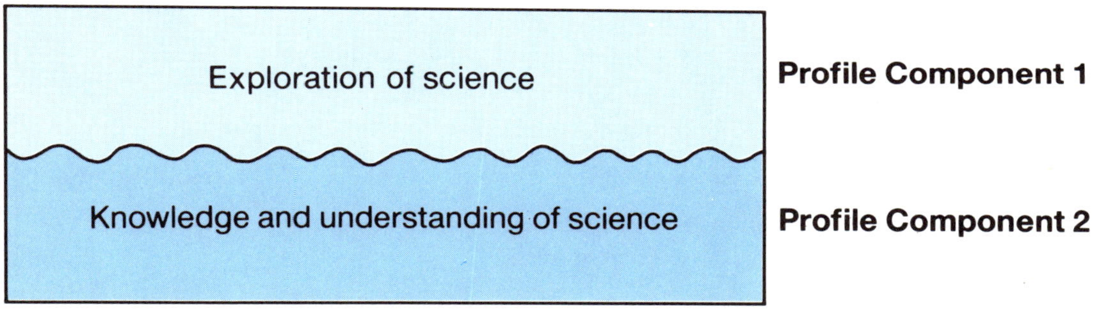

Each Profile Component is of equal importance at the first Key Reporting Stage (age 7) and of almost equal importance at the second (age 11).

The Profile Components in the Science Curriculum are not divided into subjects, like the maths and English curricula are. In science, 4 of the 5 Attainment Targets are concerned with scientific knowledge and skills and are grouped into one Profile Component. The other Profile Component contains only one Attainment Target which is said to be the foundation for the other four Attainment Targets 2 – 5. Each of these Attainment Targets attempts to ensure a child's progress through a particular area of scientific knowledge.

When it comes to work in the classroom these two aspects of the Science Curriculum will be linked together – so the children are learning to explore and communicate at the same time as learning and using scientific knowledge and skills.

Isn't science too difficult for primary school children?

The science that will be taught to children at primary school is set within the everyday experiences of those children. Although science sounds hard, we must not imagine five year olds wearing white coats and juggling test tubes over bunsen burners! It is surprising just how much science comes out of daily routines; we observe how long things take to boil or cool down, we watch animals and babies developing as they grow, we are aware of the seasons, the weather and so on.

LEVEL	STATEMENTS OF ATTAINMENT
1	• know that there is a wide variety of living things, which includes human beings.
2	• know that plants and animals need certain conditions to sustain life. • understand how living things are looked after and be able to treat them with care and consideration.
3	• be able to recognise similarities and differences among living things. • be able to sort living things into broad groups according to observable features. • know that living things respond to seasonal and daily changes.
4	• be able to name the major organs and organ systems in flowering plants and mammals. • be able to assign organisms to their major groups using keys and observable features. • understand that the survival of plants and animals in an environment depends on successful competition for scarce resources. • understand food chains as a way of representing feeding relationships in an ecosystem.

These examples from Science Attainment Target 2 show how the approach to content in the science curriculum is based around everyday experiences and familiar happenings.

In the past, some primary school children have received absolutely no scientific education, and substantial numbers of pupils, especially girls, have been reluctant to choose science subjects at GCSE level and above. The National Curriculum requirement to study science from age 5 onwards will perhaps be the first step in producing a generation of science-literate adults.

FOUNDATION SUBJECTS

As we have already seen, the new curriculum is divided into the three Core subjects (maths, English and science) and seven **Foundation** subjects. These are history, geography, design and technology, music, art, PE, a modern foreign language (for 11-16 age group) and Welsh (for non-Welsh speaking schools in Wales).

Each subject has had a report produced by a working group, which consists of a panel of experts including industrialists, educationalists, and practitioners. The document that they produced outlines the subject content as it shall be defined under the National Curriculum. Some subjects, noteably history and geography, have been the focus of lively debate. However, the final curriculum documents have all been laid out in the same way. Each subject is divided into Attainment Targets and arranged in ten levels of attainment.

Cross-Curricular Work

Many of us remember lessons from our own school days. These were often divided under the various subject headings – a history lesson, a maths lesson and so on. Even in the primary school, subjects tended to be distinct although they were often taught by the same teacher.

With ten basic subjects in the National Curriculum, teachers and others in education were concerned that there would be over 50 Attainment Targets! This would make the record keeping and assessment requirements of the National Curriculum almost impossible to carry out effectively. The D.E.S. has therefore advised that the Foundation Subject Working Groups laid out the content in 5 or less ATs per subject.

Nevertheless, it would be impossible to cover all these subject areas one after the other, especially in the primary classroom. It is suggested that teachers develop different aspects of the foundation subjects through the use of a topic or project.

Integrated Work

Working in this way, teachers integrate or link the various subject disciplines through a focus upon a particular **topic.**

For example a whole school may decide to focus a term's work upon the topic of "WASTE". This will involve all sorts of approaches, from a study of Conservation and Eco-systems in the top juniors, to a sorting of rubbish in the infants.

An infant teacher in the school could organise her topic work so that it covered the following Attainment Targets:

Maths	Attainment Targets:	1	2	4	5
	Level:	1/2	1/2	1/2/3	1/2
English	Attainment Targets:	1	2	3	
	Level:	1/2/3	1/2	1/2	
Science	Attainment Targets:	2	3	5	
	Level:	1/2	1/2/3/4	1/2	

The Topic work will also cover Attainment Targets in geography and history.

Work in PE, technology, art and music could be linked to the class work on WASTE. It is possible that for some of the Foundation subjects only guidelines will be issued.

The advantages of integrated work can be easily perceived.

1. It would be impossible to teach this range of subjects and subject areas consecutively.
2. Children are encouraged to see the connections between the different subjects and to relate one piece of knowledge to another as they learn.
3. Each subject reinforces the next. Children will be practising and using similar skills across a range of subjects and so gaining confidence and expertise.
4. Individual children's interests can be catered for and encouraged. Within the structure of the work as a whole, it is possible for each child to develop his or her own pathway and follow particular enthusiasms. Any specialism a child or a group of children develop can be used to enrich the experiences of the whole class.

Will children learn enough geography and history if these are taught in an integrated fashion?

It is important to remember that the divisions between the subjects are not set in stone or clearly defined. Most experts agree that it is very difficult to separate the different subject disciplines. When is a study of the weather geography and when is it science? Is handling data and drawing graphs maths or science?

It does not matter if young children cannot label a particular piece of learning as "history" or "geography". What is important under the National Curriculum is that they cover the content outlined in the subject documents. Because children are entitled to receive a broad curriculum, teachers must demonstrate that they are addressing a reasonable spread of Attainment Targets at all the appropriate levels.

Topic work looks too easy. Is it stimulating enough for a bright child?

Although Topic work may **look** easy, a brief acquaintanceship with this way of working will show how demanding it really is for both teachers and children. Children must make connections between one piece of learning and another. They have to transfer the skills acquired in maths to science and geography and vice-versa. They have to familiarise themselves with a wide range of information. This is much more demanding than learning one isolated fact after another. Integrated work of this kind is often the best possible preparation primary children can have for their secondary education and the GCSE examinations.

Religious Education

ERA stipulates that schools must provide two things:

1. Religious Education as a part of each child's curriculum entitlement.
2. A daily act of collective worship.

This act of worship is to be broadly Christian in character, although ERA states that it should also be **non-denominational.** The Religious Education is also required to avoid any particular catechism or formulae.

Parents may decide to withdraw their children from one or both of these. Each LEA will set up a Standing Advisory Council which will advise schools on how these basic provisions may be modified in special cases. For example, in a school where a substantial proportion of the families are of a faith other than Christian, schools are allowed to modify the requirements to meet the religious needs of their communities.

Religious Education will not be subject to national guidelines or assessment.

REPORTING BACK TO PARENTS

Under the Education Reform Act parents are entitled to receive a great deal of information about their children's education. This will be given to parents under a system of *"Reporting Back"*. The diagram shows how the information will reach you from the teacher.

Reporting Back Procedures.

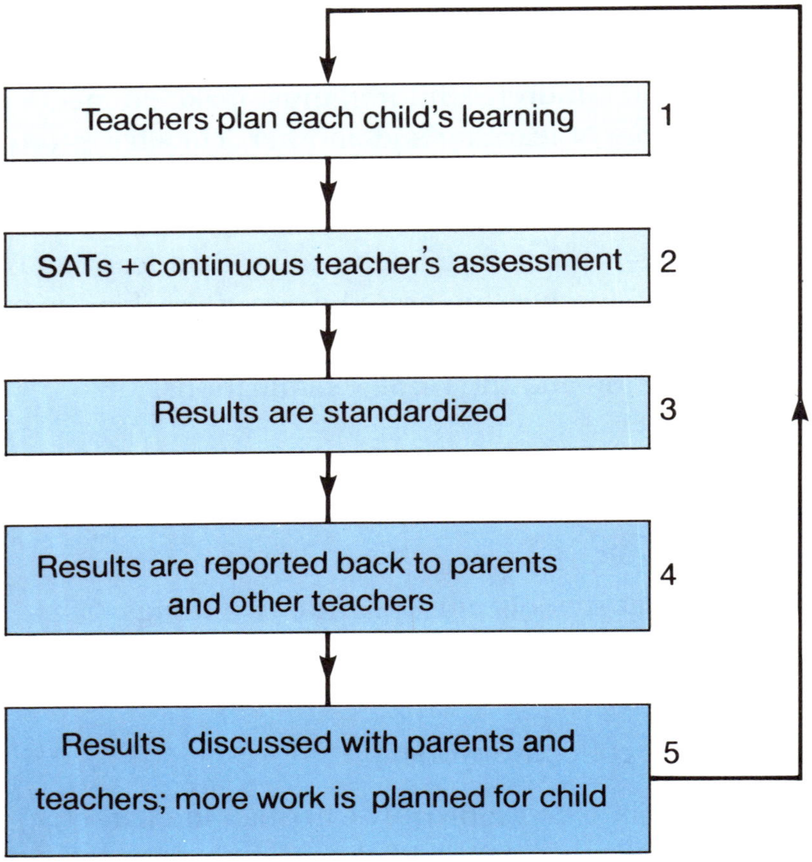

Curriculum Planning

Parents are entitled to know what teachers are planning to teach and which aspects of the Core and Foundation subjects they intend to cover during the term or year. Some schools will automatically write out a *Scheme of Work* – that is, the work planned for the term – and send it home to the parents. Almost all teachers will inform parents of the topic areas which they are studying, and which subjects these address. Teachers must supply parents with information concerning any assessments which will occur during the year, and the details of any SATs which will affect their child.

Children's Attainment on Assessments

You will also have a right to receive the outcome of any assessments of your child. You will be able to discuss these results with the teacher in detail. The Levels of Attainment presented will be related to the different Profile Components, i.e. a child will be described as being at a particular level in reading, at a particular, perhaps different level in writing, depending on the child's development of that skill, and so on.

Putting sets of results together to form an overall picture for an individual child is neither helpful nor meaningful. We do not, as parents or teachers, need to know that a child is a "level 2 child". What we do need to know are her areas of strength or weakness; for example, that she is good at reading and number work, bad at spatial awareness and writing. It is in the light of this information that a suitable Scheme of Work for the child's subsequent learning can be organised.

Attainment results for a whole class or school

In all subject areas information on the Attainment of a whole class or school will be publicly available either directly through the school or indirectly through the Local Education Authority. Individual children's results go to individual parents and are not available for public scrutiny. Therefore there is no question of a 'league table' of named children in any one class or year. However, parents do have the right to be able to make comparisons between how their child is doing and the progress of the class as a whole. The results of any one class may be published as a set of distributions.

Comparing Attainment levels for one class

	Level 1	Level 2	Level 3
Class 2 Elizabeth School, Waterloo	17%	68%	15%

These are fictitious examples only.

Or class teachers may present more generalised statements about the results in the course of a conversation or an interview with a parent; "Fred is doing well in his maths. His Level of Attainment is level 2, and he is well up with the class average. However, in reading, he is only level 1, which is disappointing since the majority of children in his class are at level 2 in this Profile Component . . ."

Will I know if my child is getting on as they should be?

The easiest and most satisfactory means of discovering in detail how your child is doing is, as always, to talk to his or her teacher. Discussing your child's actual performance in each Profile Component is the best way of finding out where he or she is succeeding and of isolating those areas where he or she may have problems and may need more attention.

The outcomes of all assessments will be most useful in that they help parents and teachers to see where a particular child's strengths and weaknesses are in specific areas of the curriculum.

Supposing my child has special educational needs, can he or she opt out of the National Curriculum?

The Education Reform Act lays down the entitlement of every child to receive a broad and balanced education. If the National Curriculum, or a part of it, is seen by those professionally concerned to be inappropriate to the needs of a particular child it is possible for the headteacher to disapply or modify the National Curriculum. This will normally be done through a Statement which covers a pupil with special educational needs. However, the emphasis of the National Curriculum is as an entitlement for all; heads should only seek to 'disapply' the National Curriculum in exceptional circumstances. Parents, of course, have a right to appeal about what is in the Statement.

Will the figures for the school as a whole help me to find out how good a school it is?

It is important to recognise that the collated results for a whole class or for a whole school will give only one indication amongst many of how well the school or teacher is doing. There are two further points to be made here:

Many factors can affect the overall figures for a class or school. E.g. in a school where a number of the parents and children are bilingual, the results of tests given in English to 7 year olds may be not a very sensible way of judging the school or the quality of the teaching.

Many other factors are important when attempting to assess how good the school is. Is the curriculum satisfactory? Are the children well-motivated and keen to learn? Is the atmosphere calm and purposeful? Is your child stimulated and interested? Do they want to go to school? Positive answers to questions such as these may give you a far more important set of criteria by which to judge the school.

Information parents should receive from schools

1. Helpful and accessible information about the work that is planned for your child over the next term or year.
2. The details of any assessments which are due to occur during that period of time and how these will affect your child.
3. The assessment outcomes – that is, a detailed report of your child's performance on all the Profile Components and Attainment Targets where necessary.
4. The necessary information to enable you to compare your child's progress with that of their peers in the rest of the class.
5. Most importantly – the chance to participate fully in your child's education through such activities as reading at home and helping with other areas of work.

In Summary

The Education Reform Act provides for a great deal of information about their children to be available to parents. This information relates both to the work a child will do and to the results of assessment. There is no doubt that the more information which is shared between parents and teachers the more satisfactory the conversations between them are likely to be. It is only when teachers and parents begin to work together in partnership that the benefits to our children's education will begin to be seen.

KEY CONCERNS

Teaching the National Curriculum

Educational psychologists have shown that learning is not like walking in a straight line or climbing a ladder. We do not all learn one thing, then another, then another, in the **same** order. It is more accurate to compare a child's learning to doing a complicated 3d jig-saw or making a complex model than climbing a ladder. We put in a couple of pieces, then we may do another section altogether. Sometimes we make a connection we hadn't seen before and occasionally we link two sections we hadn't previously realised could be joined.

The National Curriculum is structured according to the ladder theory of learning and there could be a danger of teachers narrowly confining themselves to teaching one rung at a time.

Assessment

It is worth emphasising the importance of concentrating on the Teacher's Report rather than the actual level in each Profile Component. For example, like Mary, a child might be good at handling data and yet particularly poor at spatial awareness. Adding the results of the two Attainment Targets for handling data and spatial awareness would in fact give an overall result that showed the child as **average** for the overall Profile Component (one very good result and one poor result would lead to an overall result in the middle). This would therefore hide the fact that the child was above average in one part of that component but below average in the other. In this way, if only the level achieved is shown, an especially poor performance giving cause for concern, could remain unnoticed.

It is also worth pointing out that any form of assessment, no matter how lengthy or detailed, can only serve a limited purpose and cannot demonstrate a child's full potential – what he or she is capable of achieving. All we can find out from assessment is what a child actually can do at any one moment. So a child may be a mathematical genius but all a particular test can tell us is that she can add numbers up to 20!

We must bear in mind that a teacher usually has between 25 and 35 children in her class. With the best will in the world, even the most gifted teacher cannot hope to make accurate assessments on each of 30 children across the great number statements of attainment that there are at level 2. If we, as teachers or parents start to believe that the National Assessment can tell us all there is to know about a child, this would be counter-productive. We could prejudge a child and thereby prejudice their chances of improvement. We could cease to allow our children to surprise us with their abilities.

Teachers

Under the National Curriculum, the teacher's role has changed considerably. Not only are teachers now expected to produce a great deal of written information concerning what they have planned and how they are going to cover the curriculum, they are also required to keep extensive records about each child's progress through each subject. Teachers are anxious to give parents information and to assess the children's progress. But they also wish to teach, and to enable children to learn and to aquire new skills.

Bilingual children

Many children today are bilingual. Although the English document mentions giving value to children's first language and to non-standard dialects, in practice, the structure of the National Curriculum works against it. Owing to the assessment at 7, many children will be under pressure to abandon their first language and to operate purely in English. Welsh bilingual children will be assessed in Welsh. However, this does not at present apply to any other language in use in England or Wales. While the learning of English remains a major priority, many people feel it would be unfair prematurely to limit a child's attainment in (say) maths, by how well he or she could respond in English.

Results

The law requires that schools publish their distributions of results for children aged 11. Although schools are not required by law to publish the results of 7 year olds, many schools will feel under pressure to do so. There may be a temptation to treat these distributions as being the main, or even the only, criterion for judging the effectiveness of a school or teacher. Results are dependent upon many different factors and causes; judgement made on this basis alone runs the danger of excellent teaching and many good schools going unrecognised. The LEA may wish to supply a statement about the school prior to publication.

SOME DO'S AND DON'TS

Here are 7 simple ways which will help parents join teachers in making the National Curriculum work in their children's interests.

1. **Avoid using assessment to label children.** Remember what assessment is there for. It is to help you diagnose a child's areas of weakness and strength better, to plan their future work. It is **not** there to enable you to attach labels to children at the ages of 11, or 14, or 16, let alone 7.

2. **Keep talking to your child's teacher.** No laws can ever enforce a good relationship between parents and teachers. Ultimately both teachers and parents care about the same thing – the progress of the child – so **keep talking.** The official information to which you are now entitled should help you to communicate better rather than replace genuine conversation.

3. **Don't make judgements based solely on results.** Remember that there are many important factors which come together to make a good school and a good classroom. A child can have a thoroughly bad or harmful experience of learning in a classroom where all the children are achieving at an above average level. Conversely, many children respond well when certain types of pressure are not too great and results are not given undue importance. It is not easy to define what makes a good school – a calm atmosphere, a sense of responsibility and discipline, stimulating teaching, a pleasant environment, a genuine acceptance and care for others, among other things.

4. **Don't expect all teaching and all classrooms to look the same.** There is now a National Curriculum which gives teachers the **content** of the curriculum. It tells teachers **what** to teach but not **how** to teach it. The way in which teachers choose to organise their classroom, their methods of teaching and the timetabling of subjects are all still left to individual choice. There will be variations in approach and classroom organisation with different teachers across different types of schools in different areas.

5. **Remember that the SATs are not like old-fashioned tests.** The Standard Assessment Tasks are only one part of the assessment of a child. Most of what they learn is assessed by means of the Teacher's Assessment. Also, the SATs are not the sort of tests for which coaching will particularly help. The

best way to help your child is to show interest and enthusiasm about what they are learning, and to share it with them. Maths games, enjoying reading together, and helping them investigate and understand the world around them will do as much good for their learning as a page of sums!

6. **Do recognise that the National Curriculum does not mean a return to old-fashioned schooling.** The National Curriculum "builds firmly on existing good practice which is itself supported to a great extent by existing books and materials". The content of the National Curriculum emphasises certain educational principles: children must be able to apply what they learn; they will learn more effectively if given plenty of opportunity to discuss what they are learning in groups; practical experiences have an essential part to play in learning any subject.

   The National Curriculum is not intended to bring about a return to bored children sitting in rows of desks facing a limited and often irrelevant curriculum in silence. It will attempt to foster the best of good educational practice as it has developed over the last 30 years.

7. **Do bear in mind that children develop at different rates and in different directions.** Children vary a great deal, not only in their rate of learning but also in the way in which they learn things. Most children develop in fits and starts rather than at a uniform pace. One child may take 8 months to learn to recognise his numbers and then learn to add up in a week; another may come to school recognising numbers up to 50 and then take a whole term to understand what addition is about. Competitiveness between parents, especially when it leads to directly comparing children, is unproductive at best and anxiety producing at worst.

GLOSSARY

AT
Attainment Target. The knowledge, skills and understanding it is expected that a child will acquire in one area of one subject during their 11 years of education.

Continuous Assessment
A teacher's on-going record of what a child is working on, and the levels at which they are working – in all subjects kept throughout a Key Stage.

Core Subjects
The Core Subjects are maths, English and science, and Welsh for Welsh-speaking schools in Wales.

Criteria
The facts and skills against which a child's performance in any one subject can be monitored.

DES
Department of Education and Science. The government department responsible for Education.

ERA
Education Reform Act. The legislation which introduced the National Curriculum.

Foundation Subjects
Technology, history, geography, music, art, PE and a modern foreign language at secondary age, and Welsh for non-Welsh speaking schools in Wales.

GCSE
General Certificate of Secondary Education. The examinations students currently take at the end of compulsory schooling at the age of 16.

Key Reporting Stage
The end of one Programme of Study and the beginning of another. The point in time at which SATs are administered and assessment results are reported. The Key Reporting Stages are at 7, 11, 14 and 16 years old.

Key Stage
This is the Programme of Study to be taught leading up to a Key Reporting Stage. The Key Stages are 5-7, 7-11, 11-14 and 14-16 years old.

LEA
Local Education Authority The regional elected body responsible for education in that area.

Level of Attainment
The Attainment Targets are divided into ten levels. Each of these is like one rung on a ten runged ladder in each subject.

NCC
National Curriculum Council. The Government appointed agency set up to advise on the delivery of the National Curriculum, and all other aspects of the curriculum in schools.

Profile Component
The areas into which each subject is divided for ease of Reporting Back.

Programme of Study
The matters, skills and processes which are to be taught at each Key Stage in each subject.

Reporting Back
The processes and procedures by which all the required information including the outcomes of assessment, is supplied to those entitled to receive it.

SAT
Standard Assessment Task. The externally supplied set of standard tasks which children will do in order to be assessed at the Key Reporting Stages.

Scheme of Work
The teachers plan of work for each individual child which is designed to enable them to progress through the levels of the National Curriculum in each subject.

SEAC
Schools Examination and Assessment Council. The Government appointed agency responsible for over-seeing the entire assessment process of the National Curriculum and all matters concerned with examinations and assessment.